ROBOTS AND AI

THIS EDITION
Editorial Management by Oriel Square
Produced for DK by WonderLab Group LLC
Jennifer Emmett, Erica Green, Kate Hale, *Founders*

Editors Grace Hill Smith, Libby Romero, Maya Myers, Michaela Weglinski;
Photography Editors Kelley Miller, Annette Kiesow, Nicole DiMella; **Managing Editor** Rachel Houghton;
Designers Project Design Company; **Researcher** Michelle Harris; **Copy Editor** Lori Merritt;
Indexer Connie Binder; **Proofreader** Larry Shea; **Reading Specialist** Dr. Jennifer Albro;
Curriculum Specialist Elaine Larson

Published in the United States by DK Publishing
1745 Broadway, 20th Floor, New York, NY 10019

Copyright © 2023 Dorling Kindersley Limited
DK, a Division of Penguin Random House LLC
23 24 25 26 10 9 8 7 6 5 4 3 2 1
001-334129-Sept/2023

A catalog record for this book
is available from the Library of Congress.
HC ISBN: 978-0-7440-7586-1
PB ISBN: 978-0-7440-7587-8

DK books are available at special discounts when purchased in bulk for sales promotions, premiums,
fundraising, or educational use. For details, contact: DK Publishing Special Markets,
1745 Broadway, 20th Floor, New York, NY 10019
SpecialSales@dk.com

Printed and bound in China

The publisher would like to thank the following for their kind permission to reproduce their images:
a=above; c=center; b=below; l=left; r=right; t=top; b/g=background

123RF.com: Baloncici 3b; **Alamy Stock Photo:** CBW 14tl, Ian Dagnall 24-25b, Dpa Picture Alliance / Julian Stratenschulte 40-41b,
Dpa Picture Alliance / Ole Spata 44-45b, Dino Fracchia 8tl, Jeremy Sutton-Hibbert 18cl, Science History Images 9tr, sharky 38tl,
US Navy Photo 42tl; **Dreamstime.com:** Alexpodoliykh 23tr, Archangel80889 36tl, Andrey Armyagov 29crb, Sven Bachstroem 38-39b,
Biletskiy 28-29t, Jerry Coli 30tl, Elinba 22-23b, Feverpitched 27tr, Glazyuk 44tl, Johnny Habell 28clb, Alexander Hasenkampf 11tr,
Nina Hilitukha 44cl, Bogdan Hoda 8-9b, Kittipong Jirasukhanont 10tl, Sergey Klopotov 25tr, Mike2focus 28tl, Monkey Business
Images 8cl, Newlight 1b, Najmi Arif Norkaman 22cl, Nuruddean 20cla, Patrick Marcel Pelz 16cl, Garn Phakathunya 30br,
Pincarel 31tr, Andrey Popov 4-5, Suwin Puengsamrong 12-13b, 26-27b, Ralwel 27cr, Robertmandel 12tl, Seaphotoart 33tr, Shoeke27 31tl,
Oleksii Spesyvtsev 24tl, Prot Tachapanit 21t, Manfred Thuerig 17crb, Alexander Tolstykh 10b, Toxawww 16tl;
Getty Images: AFP / Boris Horvat / Staff 39tr, Andreas Solaro / AFP 32-33b, Daniel Leal / AFP 15cr, Dirk Waem / Belga Mag / AFP
43tr, Mark Ralston / AFP 35tr, Yasser Al-Zayyat / AFP 16-17r, Bettmann 19tr, 19bl, Carla Gottgens / Bloomberg 6clb, David Paul Morris
/ Bloomberg 30cl, Corbis Historical 20b, Thierry Falise / LightRocket 26tl, Moment / Jia Yu 14-15b, Beata Zawrzel / NurPhoto 34tl,
Michel Porro 22tl, Stone / Dana Neely 34-35b, Chung Sung-Jun / Staff 45tr, The Image Bank / Chris Rogers 42-43b;
Getty Images / iStock: E+ / Marco VDM 15tr, eternalcreative 12clb; **NASA:** JPL-Caltech 36br, 37t, 37cra, JSC 32clb;
Science Photo Library: Hank Morgan 6tl; **Shutterstock.com:** Gorodenkoff 11b, Jenson 7tl
Cover images: *Front:* **Shutterstock.com:** sdecoret

All other images © Dorling Kindersley
For more information see: www.dkimages.com

For the curious
www.dk.com

ROBOTS AND AI

Roxanne Troup

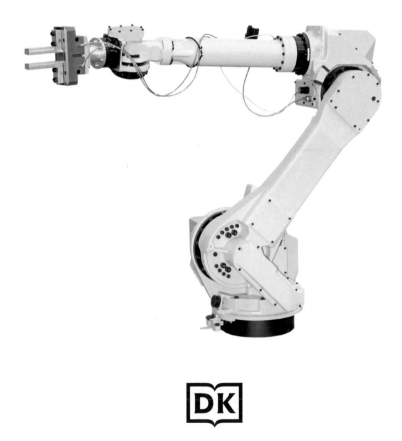

DK

CONTENTS

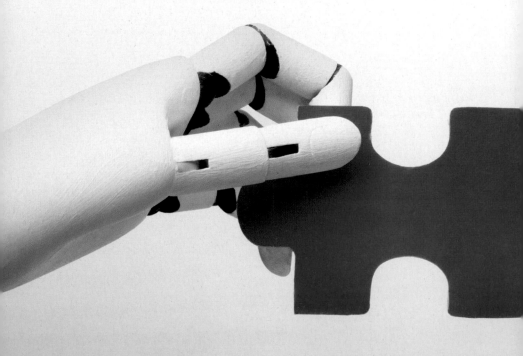

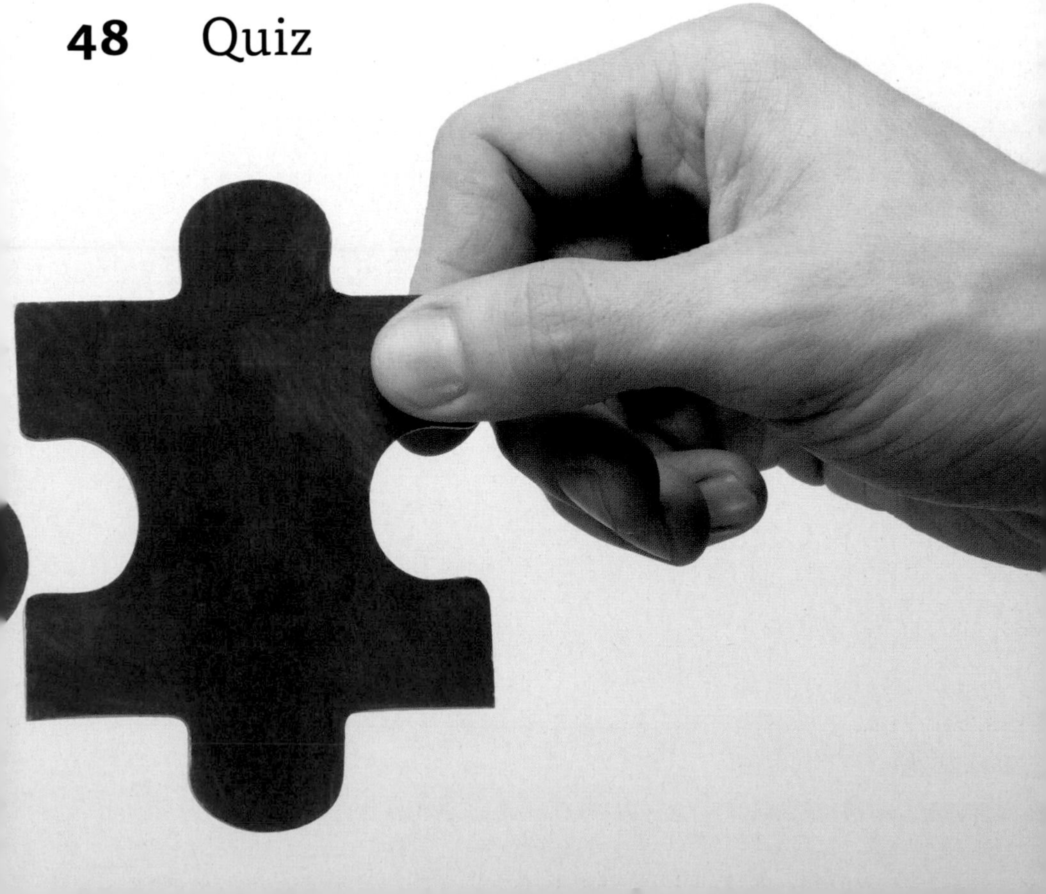

Microbots
Robots vary in size. Really small robots, like the one above, are called microbots. The smallest microbot so far is less than 0.04 inches (1 mm) long. That's about as thin as the edge of a credit card.

Mega Robot
Considered by some to be the world's largest robot, this fleet of trains hauls iron ore across Western Australia. The fleet is 1.5 miles (2.4 km) long and can drive itself.

AMAZING ROBOTS

What do you imagine when someone says the word "robot"? Do you picture a human-like machine that walks with stiff arms and talks in a mechanical voice? Robots like that do exist. But most robots don't look like people. Robots come in different shapes and sizes to fit the type of work they do.

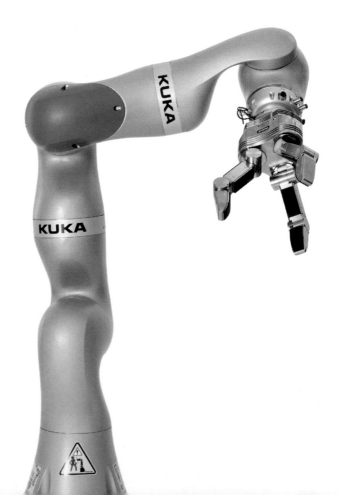

Some robots look like giant arms. They work in factories, doing things like building cars or wrapping candy bars. Others look like tiny tanks. They roll through rubble to find survivors after an earthquake.

Robots can do just about anything. They might explore the ocean or fly over a sports game to take pictures. Robots also clean carpets, work in hospitals, and surprise you at amusement parks.

More Than Machines
All robots are machines. But not all machines are robots. Machines, such as toasters, help people do tasks quicker and easier. But these machines must have someone to operate them. Once programmed, robots do their jobs without help.

Word Origins
The word "robot" comes from a Slavic word that means "forced work." The term was first used in a play from the 1920s. In the play, a company built its own workers called robots.

Sewer Bots
People began using robots to inspect, clean, and repair sewers in the 1970s.

Roboticists
Engineers who design and build robots are called roboticists.

Dirty, dangerous, and delicate jobs are good fits for robots. Robots often do jobs and go places people can't. They may lift heavy car parts or fly into a tornado to collect data. Robots also do jobs some people don't want to do, like inspect smelly sewers. Cameras on a sewer bot show workers where to fix a pipe.

Robots are the perfect workers for dull jobs that repeat the same motions over and over. They do their jobs without getting bored or making mistakes. And they work really fast. Gum-wrapping robots can wrap up to 2,500 pieces of gum per minute.

All day long, assembly line robots move and prepare small pieces of chocolate.

Hazardous Duty
Volcano bots explore inside Earth's volcanoes. Their discoveries help scientists understand volcanoes on Earth and other planets.

Lab Bots
Some robots test computer programs, which are the series of steps computers take to solve problems. This helps roboticists improve designs and develop new technologies.

A Big Impact
There are millions of robots working throughout the world.

HOW ROBOTS WORK

Robots are machines designed to do specific tasks without help. They have sensors to collect information about their environment. A controller inside the robot uses that information to tell the robot what to do. The controller is run by a computer program.

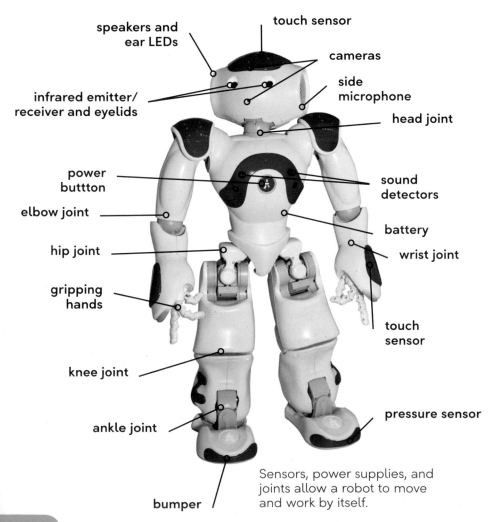

speakers and ear LEDs

touch sensor

cameras

infrared emitter/ receiver and eyelids

side microphone

head joint

power buttton

sound detectors

elbow joint

battery

hip joint

wrist joint

gripping hands

touch sensor

knee joint

pressure sensor

ankle joint

bumper

Sensors, power supplies, and joints allow a robot to move and work by itself.

Programs are written in special computer language called code. Code breaks a big problem or task into small step-by-step instructions a computer can follow.

For example, you can't tell a robot to make a sandwich—it doesn't know how. Instead, you create lines of code that tell the robot to lay two pieces of bread side-by-side. More code tells the robot to open a jar of peanut butter, pick up a knife, and use the knife to scoop peanut butter out of the jar. The code keeps giving the robot instructions, one step at a time, until the sandwich is finished.

Operator Error
Errors in computer codes are called bugs.

First Steps
The first programming language was called FORTRAN. It was developed in 1964, and is still being used today.

A robot needs an energy source to power its movements, sensors, and controllers. Most robots are powered by electricity. They can be plugged into an outlet or use electrical energy stored in a battery. There are robots that get their energy from gasoline generators or solar power, too.

In many ways, robots are similar to people. Robot gears function like human joints. Gears allow the robot to move. Sensors collect information, like your senses do. Camera sensors let robots "see" where they are going.

Microphones let robots "hear." Other sensors tell robots when they bump into something. Some robots even have sensors to "smell" the air.

Robot sensors measure temperature, speed, distance, and force. Sensors can tell a robot if a light is on or if the robot is off-balance.

Elmer and Elsie
In 1948, William Grey Walter was studying the human brain when he started to work on the tortoise-shaped robots called Elmer and Elsie. They used light and touch sensors to steer themselves.

The battery pack on a greenhouse robot, which moves plants around a nursery, can last four to six hours per charge.

Laying the Foundation
British mathematician Alan Turing is known as the founder of AI. He thought if people could use information to make choices and solve problems, computers could, too. He developed a test for artificial intelligence called the Turing test. Roboticists still use his test today.

WHAT IS ARTIFICIAL INTELLIGENCE?

In some robots, controllers use data from sensors to choose the robot's next set of actions. This is called artificial intelligence, or AI. Artificial intelligence is technology that sorts data the same way a human brain does.

Regular computer programs follow a series of steps to complete each task. The steps can't be reordered or changed without reprogramming the computer. Artificial intelligence is different. AI robots "think" through several actions at once, and then choose the best action to complete a task.

AI is not limited to robotics. The map feature on a smartphone uses AI to give directions. But the phone is not a robot. It can't complete tasks—like driving to your friend's house—on its own.

A navigation app uses AI technology to sort through all the possible routes you could take to get somewhere. It chooses the fastest one.

AI and Health
Fitness trackers monitor your heart rate and other vital signs. These devices use AI to alert people of health risks and help them make better health choices.

Personal Helper
Someday, everyone may have a basket robot to carry their stuff. These robots use AI to identify their owner and follow them around. They can carry up to 40 pounds (18 kg) of cargo.

On the Surface
Sophia's "skin" is called Frubber®. This special type of rubber looks and moves a bit like human skin.

Spreading the Word
Sophia can recreate 62 different facial expressions. The robot speaks English and Mandarin Chinese and can say a few phrases in other languages as well.

AI is amazing, but not everyone trusts it. Some people think AI will take their jobs. Others worry that robots could be used to harm people. And some people are afraid AI will become so smart that humans won't be able to control it. But don't worry. All robots, even robots with artificial intelligence, can only do what they are programmed to do.

Roboticists created Sophia in 2016 to help people understand AI technology. They made Sophia look a bit like a real person so people wouldn't be afraid of it. They programmed Sophia to make eye contact and recognize languages, too. These abilities make it easier for people to connect with Sophia. Sophia has traveled to more than 25 countries to give speeches about technology and its role in society.

Citizen Sophia
In 2017, Sophia became an honorary citizen of Saudi Arabia. Sophia is the first robot to be granted citizenship in a country.

EARLY BOTS

Hundreds of years before computers or artificial intelligence existed, robot-like machines called automata captured people's imaginations. Clockmakers and engineers built them to amuse kings and important guests. A series of springs, levers, weights, and gears made the machines move.

One popular automata, a "digesting" duck, was created by French inventor Jacques de Vaucanson. The duck flapped its wings, "ate" grain, and dropped waste pellets out its backside. The duck didn't really digest anything. The food it "ate" collected in a container inside the duck. The pellets it dropped were preloaded.

By the early 1900s, true robots were invented. They ran on electricity. The wires needed to connect that electricity to all their moving parts took up a lot of space. One of the first electric robots was seven feet (2.1 m) tall and weighed 265 pounds (120 kg). Its name was Elektro.

In 1939, Elektro awed visitors at the World's Fair. Elektro's system of gears and motors allowed it to walk, move its body, and "speak."

Elektro "spoke" 700 different words. Inside its body, a telephone handset "heard" voice commands before playing a recorded response.

Robot's Best Friend
Elektro was so popular that it was joined by a robotic dog named Sparko the following year. Sparko could bark, sit, and beg.

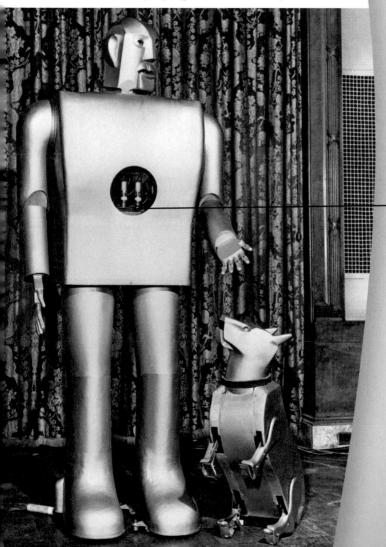

It's Real!
Elektro's inventor cut a hole in the robot's chest to prove that no human was inside.

In 1995, 50 years after World War II ended, students at the University of Pennsylvania recreated ENIAC using newer technology. All of the computer's programming fit on a computer chip the size of a bottle cap like this one.

In 1946, the US Army completed construction on first programmable electronic computer. They called it ENIAC—the Electronic Numerical Integrator and Computer. A team of female mathematicians programmed ENIAC to solve math problems for the US military.

Operating this all-electric computer wasn't as simple as typing on a keyboard. Every time ENIAC needed to solve a different type of equation, the mathematicians had to reprogram it.

ENIAC was so large that it filled an entire room.

Integrated circuits calculate and store information.

Reprogramming involved pulling out the wires and connecting them in a different order so ENIAC would follow a different series of steps to solve a new problem.

Fifteen years later, small computer chips—called integrated circuits—were invented. Instead of wires and tubes, integrated circuits used thin sheets of metal to create a path for electricity to travel. The chips allowed engineers to build smaller computers and robots that were able to complete more complicated jobs. Thanks to that invention, roboticists have created all the different types of robots we use today.

A Giant Brain

The press called ENIAC a "giant brain." ENIAC could solve 5,000 addition problems in one second.

Wonder Women

The real brains behind ENIAC's success were its six female programmers: Frances Bilas, Elizabeth Jean Jennings, Ruth Lichterman, Kathleen McNulty, Frances Elizabeth Snyder, and Marlyn Wescoff.

Keeping Beaches Clean
Robots don't just clean indoors. Beach-cleaning robots sift through sand and collect trash as they roll along.

Cleaning Rivers
Robotic boats help clean Earth's rivers. As trash floats toward the boat, a solar-powered conveyor belt pulls it out of the water.

DOMESTIC BOTS

We use many different kinds of robots today. Domestic robots do chores around the house. Some domestic robots vacuum dirt off the floor. Others crawl up and down windows, spraying cleaner and scrubbing the windows clean. Some mow the lawn, and some even scrub the sides and bottom of a pool. All you have to do is empty the dirt and trash they collect.

Companies are even developing robots than can do all the cooking.

A robot chef is programmed to copy a human chef's movements, which were recorded while preparing a meal.

In some cases, the arms of a robotic chef hang from a track on the ceiling. The track lets the robot move to different areas in the kitchen.

Other kinds of domestic robots help people care for themselves. They may remind people to take their medicine, do some exercise, or even help them get out of bed. A medicine-dispensing robot sits on a counter and holds medicine. When it's time for your next dose, the robot reminds you and drops the correct amount of medicine into a cup.

Guarding Your Home
Some people use alarm systems to protect their homes. Others prefer guard dogs. Another option is a dog-like robot. It has built-in cameras to scan a home's surroundings. With other attachments, it can open doors and pick up things for you.

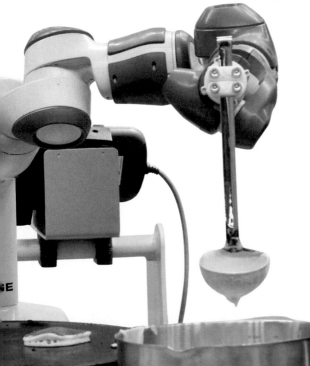

ENTERTAINMENT BOTS

Most entertainment robots are toys. Many of these robots use AI to play learning games with users. The robots might teach someone another language or help them learn to code. These robots come with special programs that allow people to communicate with them using a tablet or smartphone. Simply tap a button to tell the robot to follow a path, spin, or flash its lights.

Teaching STEM
Many teachers use entertainment robots to help students learn STEM skills like coding. STEM stands for science, technology, engineering, and mathematics.

This *T. rex* may look real, but it's a giant animatronic robot that is operated by remote control.

There are entertainment robots at museums and amusement parks, too. Animatronics are life-like robot-puppets. They bring favorite movie characters to life and let people "talk" to famous people from history.

An animatronic robot has a metal frame. Over the frame, designers build a puppet out of foam. The foam is covered with a rubbery "skin" that bends and moves with the robot. Animatronics are controlled remotely or programmed to respond to motion sensors.

A Pet for All
Are you allergic to furry pets? A robotic dog will play games and learn tricks without making you sneeze. And it doesn't need to eat.

Introducing Animatronics
The Walt Disney Company was one of the first businesses to use animatronics. The Enchanted Tiki Room, displaying animatronic birds, opened at Disneyland in 1962. A few years later, similar robots appeared in the film *Mary Poppins.*

FLYING BOTS

Flying robots are called drones. Drones are uncrewed aerial vehicles, or UAVs. This means they don't have pilots on board. Some drones are programmed to fly on their own using GPS to find their way. Others need people to steer them or change their speed with a remote control. A motor inside the drone spins blades that lift the drone into the air, like a helicopter.

Tiny Flyer
One of the smallest robots in the world looks like a tiny bee. It's only half the size of a paper clip. Roboticists created it with AI technology, hoping it would learn to cooperate with similar robots. Someday, these tiny flyers may help pollinate crops or monitor the weather.

People use drones to do many different things. Farmers use drones to take care of their fields. After a storm, they fly drones over their fields to check for crop damage. During the growing season, drones help monitor crops to ensure the plants stay healthy. Ranchers use drones, too. Drones help them find and even herd cattle on big ranches. Cattle tend to move away from the sound of a large drone. This helps ranchers move cattle to different pastures.

Sensors on an agricultural drone measure soil moisture and temperature in a field. Farmers use that information to plan when and how to water crops.

Delivery Drone
Businesses use drones to deliver packages to people's homes. The business programs the drone with the delivery address before it flies. Then, the drone uses GPS to navigate.

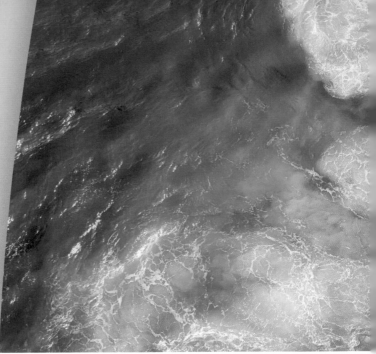

New Firefighters
A Chinese company is testing a large drone that shoots fire-extinguishing "bombs" to put out skyscraper fires.

Drones are often used to take pictures and video from the air. Photography drones can be deployed quickly and without the need for expensive helicopters or airplanes. They can also fly in places large machines can't, making them important tools in search-and-rescue operations.

Many photography drones are small. Their batteries are also small, so they can't fly long without recharging. Bigger jobs require bigger drones with longer flight times.

Drones make aerial photography easier.

The MQ-9A Reaper flies more than 27 hours. Soldiers use it to spy on their enemies. A computer operator, called a pilot, controls the Reaper from far away. Satellites use radio signals to connect the computer to the drone. GPS tells the pilot where the drone is. Cameras on the drone show the pilot what the drone sees.

Rescuers use drones to find people when they're lost. Bright lights shine down so searchers can see in the dark. Infrared cameras detect body heat. Video cameras record from above. The data helps rescuers see large areas.

Big Drones for Big Jobs
The world's largest drone, the Ravn X, is designed to launch satellites into space.

INDUSTRIAL BOTS

Industrial robots are designed for use in factories. These robots are very precise and can do the same job over and over without getting tired. The first factory robot was put to work in 1961. Shaped like a giant arm, it welded car parts together. Today, industrial robots often do jobs that are too difficult or dangerous for people to do.

Small but Mighty
Though small as a suitcase, warehouse robots can lift up to 1,000 pounds (454 kg).

Industrial robots do everything from building computers to packing boxes for shipping.

Some cobots turn themselves off when people are nearby to keep worksites safe.

Industrial robots can work 24 hours a day. But they are often very large. It's not always safe for them to work near people. So, roboticists designed a solution—cobots.

Cobots are collaborative robots. They are smaller and lighter than other industrial robots and have extra sensors. Cobots use AI technology to understand information from their sensors. This allows them to monitor their surroundings. When people are nearby, cobots adjust their speed or force to keep people safe.

Getting the Word Out
Designers of Unimate, the first factory robot, used television to get the word out about their invention. In 1966, the robotic arm wowed viewers on *The Tonight Show* by hitting a golf ball into a cup and conducting the band.

Heavy-Duty Work
The world's strongest robot can lift 5,000 pounds (2,300 kg).

Learning from Robots
Pepper is a humanoid cobot that talks. Researchers hope Pepper's self-talk will reveal more about the way computers solve problems.

Work in Progress
Robonaut 2 is still learning to use all of its limbs and sensors. Eventually, it could help astronauts clean the ISS and make space station repairs.

HUMANOIDS

Everything on the International Space Station (ISS)—its cabin space and its controls and equipment—was created with astronauts in mind. So, when scientists developed Robonaut 2 to help astronauts onboard, they designed the robot to look and move like a person.

Robonaut 2 is a humanoid robot. Most humanoids have a head, chest, and arms. They may walk on legs or roll around on wheels. Some humanoids even have hand-like grippers to pick up objects.

Work for some humanoids looks like play. Every year since 1997, robotic teams from around the world have gathered to compete in the RoboCup. This fun competition lets scientists test and improve their robots' skills. For instance, if a robot gets distracted by other moving objects as it runs after a ball, the scientist knows its code needs to be more specific. If the robot falls while trying to kick the ball, the scientist knows to adjust the sensor that controls balance.

In Deep Water
To help explore the ocean, scientists created a humanoid submarine that swims using propellers. This virtual diving assistant has sensors in its hands that let human controllers "feel" what the robot touches.

MEDICAL BOTS

Medical robots can be found in nursing homes and hospitals. They may care for the elderly or deliver supplies. One medical robot rolls into hospital rooms and shines a bright ultraviolet light. The light kills germs and helps keep the hospital clean.

Medical robots help doctors perform surgery, too. Doctors use a computer to control the robot's arms. Tiny cameras on each arm show the doctor what the robot is doing.

A surgical robot is a type of cobot.

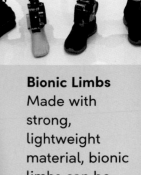

With surgical robots, doctors work faster and make smaller cuts on their patients. This helps patients heal quicker.

Bionic prosthetics are another type of medical robot. These robots replace missing or injured body parts. The bionic parts have sensors that read messages from the wearer's brain. This makes the robot move like a part of the body.

Bionic Limbs
Made with strong, lightweight material, bionic limbs can be used for anything the wearer wants to do—run, dance, catch a baseball, or bake cookies.

Cute Helper
Soft robotic seals use AI to respond to touch and sound. In nursing homes, the robot remembers who interacts with it and "cries" when it isn't getting enough attention. This helps the robot form a connection with the person using it.

A Technology Surprise
Scientists created Curiosity to explore Mars for at least one Martian year, which is 687 Earth days. But it has been steadily working for over 10 years—longer than anyone thought possible.

First Martian Rover
NASA has sent several rovers to explore Mars. The first, Sojourner, arrived in 1997. It took photos of the Martian surface. Its instruments studied what Martian rocks and dirt were made of.

SCIENTIFIC BOTS

Scientific robots help people explore and study Earth and beyond. Some of the most familiar—and famous—scientific robots are rovers.

A rover is a science laboratory on wheels. It has robotic arms that pick up and collect samples, sensors for taking measurements, and cameras that take photos for the rover to send back to Earth.

Curiosity is a rover that explores our neighboring planet Mars. It landed on the Red Planet in 2012.

Curiosity

Ingenuity

Perseverance

Perseverance and Ingenuity are conducting experiments on Mars that may pave the way for humans to someday travel there.

Curiosity's mission is to test rock samples to see if life could have ever existed on Mars. Every sol, or Mars day, Curiosity sends messages back to NASA about what it has discovered.

In 2021, Curiosity was joined by another space rover named Perseverance and a mini robotic helicopter called Ingenuity. Perseverance is collecting rock samples for future scientists to study. It's also testing ways to make oxygen and searching for signs of ancient microbial life on Mars. Ingenuity is helping Perseverance navigate and teaching scientists about flying through Mars's thin atmosphere.

Upgrading for Answers
Perseverance has an onboard microphone, which allowed scientists to record the first sounds humans have ever heard from another planet.

Scientists use other scientific robots to explore and study the ocean. Underwater ROVs, or remotely operated vehicles, can dive deeper than humans can. They can also stay underwater for longer periods of time. Most ROVs have collecting arms and sensors to take measurements and samples underwater.

As an ROV swims around a hot underwater volcano, for example, its sensors measure the ocean's temperature and depth.

Comparing Dives
ROV dives usually last eight hours. Most human divers with scuba equipment can only stay underwater safely for 60 minutes. Austrian Herbert Nitsch holds the record for the longest human dive without scuba equipment. He can hold his breath for more than nine minutes!

An ROV also takes pictures of the creatures that live near the volcano's vents. Scientists use this information to map the ocean floor and discover new species.

Pencil-shaped ROVs can even explore under ice. This shape helps them conserve energy and fit through small cracks in the ice. Scientists use these robots to study glaciers in Antarctica. This helps them understand how the ice is changing and when a glacier could collapse.

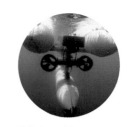

Diving Deep
Autosubs are robotic submarines that dive up to 3.7 miles (6 km) deep and can stay underwater for several months. Autosubs can explore extreme environments where it is not safe for humans to go.

Some scientific robots are built to look or behave like animals. This is called biomimicry. Biomimicry means to copy, or mimic, designs from nature. In robotics, biomimicry helps researchers understand how animals move so they can improve the ways robots move.

Think about a snake. A snake-like robot uses multiple joints to bend and twist through small, uneven spaces—just like a real snake slithers over rocks. Someday, robots like this may be used to search through rubble and find earthquake survivors.

Developing New Technology
Roboticists recently created a robot without any hard parts—that means no wires or batteries. It looks a bit like a tiny octopus and uses chemical reactions to move. They hope this "octopus" will help them create more comfortable prosthetics in the future.

Biomimicry also helps scientists improve how robots use energy. For example, a group of scientists watched kangaroos jump. They discovered that a kangaroo's legs recycle energy. Each time the kangaroo lands, its legs bend like a spring and collect energy the kangaroo uses on its next jump. Roboticists built a bionic kangaroo to do the same thing. The energy released on each bounce helps push the robot back up.

Inspired by Nature
Scientists have learned a lot from studying geckos. After examining gecko toes, they developed a nonslip material that allows robots to crawl up walls. Studying how geckos jump from tree to tree is leading to new ways for flying robots to land on vertical surfaces.

This bionic kangaroo also has a long tail, just like a real kangaroo. The tail helps keep the robot balanced.

Ghost Swimmer
Some swimming robots look and move like fish to patrol the oceans. Cameras built into the robot's body help the user see underwater.

SECURITY BOTS

Security robots keep people and property safe. They roam quietly looking for danger. If these robots sense anything odd, they sound an alarm or call the police. Most security bots use cameras to interact with their surroundings. But they move in different ways. Some roll on wheels or tracks, and others fly. One security bot even swims.

Security robots come in all shapes and sizes.

Some security robots patrol parks and neighborhoods. These police-like robots use video to monitor their surroundings and prevent crime. They can answer questions and give people directions. Some even have a "Report an Emergency" button for people to call the police.

Small tank-like robots search for bombs. Their tracks roll over rough ground while a camera sends images back to the operator, who is a safe distance away. Together, the robot and operator can disarm a bomb before it hurts anyone.

Mall Patrol
Security bots now patrol airports, malls, and other places. Data recorded by the bots may be used as evidence in courts, too.

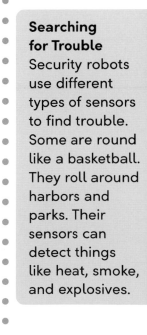

Searching for Trouble
Security robots use different types of sensors to find trouble. Some are round like a basketball. They roll around harbors and parks. Their sensors can detect things like heat, smoke, and explosives.

Teeny Robots
A nanobot would be smaller than the period at the end of a sentence.

Become a Roboticist
In college, roboticists study math, science, design, and computer programming. Roboticists are good at thinking creatively to solve problems, and they come up with new ideas for robots all the time.

ROBOTS OF THE FUTURE

As artificial intelligence improves, future robots will be able to do even more delicate and complicated jobs. Their movements will become more human-like, and they will be better able to understand their surroundings. Future robots will need less human input and could help us solve big problems like pollution and disease.

Robotic ants are one example. They are swarm robots that use radio waves to communicate with each other. They work together to move large blocks of wood across a table. Someday, this technology could be used by bigger robots to build bridges or clean up oil spills.

Nanobots are another emerging technology. They would be injected into the bloodstream and programmed to deliver medicine to specific cells.

The possibilities for robotics and AI are endless. Today, robots help with the simplest tasks. Tomorrow, they may be able to help in the most difficult situations. So, dream on, and dream big. Life as we know it is about to change.

Ideas for Robots Inspired by movies like *Robocop* and *Terminator*, Method-2 is a huge robot about the size of a female hippo (if it stood on two legs). It could be used to clean areas too dangerous for humans to enter. A pilot sits safely inside a sealed cockpit.

GLOSSARY

Animatronics
Life-like robots

Artificial intelligence
Technology that sorts data the same way a human brain does

Automata
Early mechanical robots that ran on gears and pulleys instead of electricity

Biomimicry
The design of products to mimic or copy things found in nature

Bionic prosthetics
Robotic limbs used to replace missing parts of the body

Cobots
Collaborative robots, or robots that work with people

Code
A computer language

Controller
A part of a robot run by a computer program that acts as the robot's "brain" and controls all the robot's movements

Drone
A flying robot

Engineer
Someone trained to design and build objects that solve problems

Humanoid
A human-shaped robot

Integrated circuit
A complete electronic circuit built on a small piece of plastic or silicon; a computer chip

Program
A series of steps written in computer language that computers follow to solve problems

Robot
A machine programmed to do a job without human help

Roboticist
An engineer who designs robots

Sensors
Devices that collect information about the environment so robots can sense their surroundings

INDEX

QUIZ

Answer the questions to see what you have learned. Check your answers in the key below.

1. What is a robot?

2. What do robots use to collect information about their environment?

3. True or False: All robots operate with artificial intelligence.

4. Which invention allowed engineers to build smaller robots that could do more complicated jobs?

5. What kind of robot does household chores?

6. What is a flying robot called?

7. What kind of robot is Robonaut 2?

8. What does artificial intelligence help robotic ants do?

1. A machine that is programmed to do a job 2. Sensors 3. False
4. The integrated circuit, or computer chip 5. A domestic bot
6. A drone 7. A humanoid 8. Swarm and work together to move things